SALT BODY SHIMMER

SALT BODY

YESYES BOOKS

ARICKA

SHIMMER

POEMS

FOREMAN

COVER ART: *ICE 3*, 2018, © LORNA SIMPSON
COURTESY THE ARTIST AND HAUSER & WIRTH
COVER & INTERIOR DESIGN: ALBAN FISCHER

ISBN 978-1-936919-75-8
PRINTED IN THE UNITED STATES OF AMERICA
LIBRARY OF CONGRESS CATALOGING-IN-PUBLICATION
DATA IS AVAILABLE UPON REQUEST.

PUBLISHED BY YESYES BOOKS
1614 NE ALBERTA ST
PORTLAND, OR 97211
YESYESBOOKS.COM

◤◣

KMA SULLIVAN, PUBLISHER
STEVIE EDWARDS, SENIOR EDITOR, BOOK DEVELOPMENT
ALBAN FISCHER, GRAPHIC DESIGNER
COLE HILDEBRAND, SENIOR EDITOR OF OPERATIONS
AMBER RAMBHAROSE, EDITOR, INSTAGRAM
ALEXIS SMITHERS, ASSISTANT EDITOR, *VINYL* & YYB FACEBOOK
PHILLIP B. WILLIAMS, COEDITOR IN CHIEF, *VINYL*
AMIE ZIMMERMAN, EVENTS COORDINATOR

CONTENTS

I

IN THE LAST ACT, OLUKÚN REMINDS YOU OF THE ORIGIN

I

Every morning is an incantation

against disappearing The dreams'

ragged room of slats shotgunning

my mouth In the yard, blades of sleep

bend between men who have happened

Once a cop Twice the dealer A soldier

Once, my sailor made a map where home

was a porch to drop his sorrow off

Sanded level, he'd smooth find me

sweating, a box of tools at my feet

The sun darkening my skin while

the window's shutter misinterprets

one softly rusted nail for comfort

snagged on the bodice of my dress

II

When I die

my legend would say what

> *From the new-worn denim between*

> *Her generous thighs, a spark cast out*

> *Upon tender brush*

> *And suddenly, ash: a new chapter*

I lick the char from my fingers

Bury nails in the garden beds

Or

> *She'd spit her snuff and boogie*

As my body bevels the sun's light

Take the jounce, beloved sag back

to bed Pluck the string of my longing

until the E almost snaps Touch the Dark's

knowing as often as crocus know spring

is coming As the knee recants an omen of rain

I know I live in the wake of seasons:

before summer shows up late, wet with

the heavy news *Chicago community is terrified*

after a fifth young woman disappeared

and a second body was found

Wonder if I can hoard enough minutes

to at least get a good hand of spades,

drink water between spliffs Between the books

counted Between reneged edicts Mistrials

Hung juries, all this—

Still, I sleep on my side

In dreams I send for my things:

satsuma, strawberries, sisters

who saw the thick metal

caked with rust and salt

off my waist What epistle

is living without a Beloved

to *You Good, Sis* to

Rather than only wails: woe after woe

after woman Harmonious dirge Purpled arms,

back Yes, my mother Her mother too

Backhand Butt-end of a gun

Who do you think you are A pomegranate

full of questions Each one ready to burst

while an ancient thing waits, takes a drag

off my breath

III

I've returned here before Salt

for a bee sting Salt to seal the flesh

Salt licked to cut the lime's sweet bite

Salt on the dotted line: mine my time,

muzzle when I can't keep still

Where my Want grows brilliant

Obsidian salt

When the nails fail:

you did not want to die Wanted

bigger than the idea of this body

IV

You thought

you an undone god

with two good hands

Enough *enough* to gather whatever fringe

of light left You recalcitrant fish

You buoy and you storm

Look deep into the sea

The sea knows everything

And forgets no one

MENARCHE MALARKEY
THE BEGINNING THE END

Neither of us were ready for it
My poor mother dealing The Talk
as the crisis came—sex and the bloom
that preceded it—like a war room
preparation She came with what she
knew: doctrines on the lathe of life,
how to hide secrets Ashamed of
the slick brown tributary, I tucked
the cotton into my pants pocket, sure
it'd be missed in the weekend wash
My poor mother, her hands full
of questions

      when did it/ why hadn't I/ the lies
falling from my mouth like dead stars
I held each cramp of shedding,
clotted tissue, scrubbed stains, hid
evidence How we're taught to think
ourselves criminal, perpetuate
elaborate hoaxes: all witches,
sinners All women, witches:
maybe If I could go back, I'd ask

what's in the blood? She'd say
of our miraculous machinery—
handing me a tampon, a divacup,
a wrench, a pick axe for this
business of ritual—listen, get to work

HYDROCEPHALUS AS A MISNOMER FOR WATER GOD

My small fingers point to the child—
paled from sun, gilded in plastic gold

moon-face Swaddled in white lace,
no bigger than a silver dollar Amongst

the shrine of grandchildren, nieces
nephews, adopted children from church—

and like any myth *Your sister* just like that
died Water on the brain I asked for her name

Tempest: a squall too small for all that Atlantic
I learned two things: I was not the first

of our line to hold a fraction of the sea's language,
salt degrading the world's fragile questions and

I am a miracle, can at least bring what little
offerings I have Give almonds, raspberry leaves,

sativa to what does not want to own me Sonar
through the sea's soft malevolence Who knows

what becomes of us once we're marine snow,
except Olúkun and they're not obligated to tell us

shit I hear their laughter and think of you
Walk on rhythm and think of you

What is Atlantis to a child born in The Wake
but iridescent, sharp as shells, ready to

open the flesh

BLUE MAGIC

Equipped from the siege it takes detangling
a tender-headed child's hair, mema arms herself

Thick-toothed comb parting fields of naps
Bushels of soft kink pulled through

rubber bands, roots grown into stalks, brown-
bound by metallic threaded black,

the click of two bright-marbled orbs Each
Saturday night we'd do this dance when

she had no room for my mother's and my libretto:
our fussing, the rafter pitch of my wail

Just right of her reach, a thin yellow promise
to pop my balled-up fists should I think

of breaking loose A thunderhead after washing,
drops of conditioner-thick water plump tufts

of crowded strands She pulled the plaits tight,
slathered my raw scalp with Blue Magic

Phyllis sings *When I Give My Love (This Time)*
I'm gonna make it last forever And perhaps

this too is how I'm wrought, the steel of being
beautiful: tears for what hands can do: wrangled

wild rind corkscrewed from the fruit, making
my grandfather's line repent but O those wayward

vines of riverine: the devil is a lie: in the name
of hot-combs, hair picks, bobby pins and satin scarves

I wonder if my mother saw herself in the schoolyard
as I smoothed down the feral edges of my hair watching

some brilliant black boy backflip across the grass.
In the morning mirror, gel on the bristles of a slender

brush, I scooped the baby hairs along my temple
into shells We drove down 7 Mile singing

Anita Baker, too early for all that heartbreak
I must have refused her kiss at least once at drop-

off At least once she must've squinted with worry
at my newfound love for adornment Her knuckles

white as she pulled away I don't remember looking back

FEAR LEAVES BEHIND ITS OWN LIE

It wasn't that bad
            He wasn't quick Was slow,
and the cane creak sticks
            He didn't finish In a dream
had you touch him where Grits were stirred
            It was a Saturday morning It was summer
Season for running He said after
            Titties gettin' big You dreamed it
The hallway Pressed your hair between two hot metal plates
            Bathroom suffocated by sweet stink
He stood inside the doorway You stood together in the dark
            backyard of the dream He's dead now
Who's Side Is It Anyway Grass megawatt as the moon
            Who sings to you from the deep
Oil cracks, sizzles Pastel peels Dreams
            him inside the doorways
Now you're grown in the car toward
            another late bar shift
After little sleep You dream again and don't
            know the truth The expert on NPR says
Fear leaves behind its own scent He reached for you
            It wasn't him who tried your mother

You learn later but can't tell the difference

             A friend says over your birthday dinner

You want chicken or steak Get Over It Who ain't been raped

             You want to spit Sometimes it's not Him but him

This ain't about desire so let's stop talking

             It's a bbq, lighten up Everything's alright

Ribs on the grill, turning, tender Which picked herbs

             to suture He points toward the yard,

There, a *gold fountain* In the dream he knows what he means

             A good man will kill for his, erect

A monument You can't run around with no bra on

             You can't run Around it was quick,

the turning Tinder Tender The dream creaks

             Primes the season for stirred mornings

Fear leaves us behind It owns some kind of lie

BETWEEN HEAVEN AND THE MOST SOUTHERN PLACE ON EARTH

for William Foreman Sr and Emmett Till

I watch my grandfather's morning fingers slip
each button in-then-out slotted cotton, sleeves

starched to gleam. Effortless magnolia, he sways
throughout the house, limbs bent by his own wind,

pooling cologne into his palms, blessing the edges of jaw,
arch of neck, having remembered less beautiful preparations

of the body. Delta men know their wine: a gift: age: temporary,
and when his mouth widens around *darling, I'm so surprised,*

it's not the promise of what a baptism might wash away,
but what a 1955 Tallahatchie River did not. Sometimes,

I forget which man lives inside my memory, push against
my waking years of him curled beneath the kitchen table,

folded over, swatting away snakes only he could see,
his howl writhing from the blows of his uncle's ghost.

When he was a boy again, too young to understand
why his shade of gorgeous made people violently uneasy.

There are few love songs for Sunflower, Yazoo, Money boys
to sing themselves to sleep. They learned ritual: a string of slow

breaths between buffing black shoes, until their lungs fill
with every fleck of light. When my grandfather pours

into his overcoat, I am young to knowing too. How fragile
his return before his musk fades from the front door.

FIELD STUDY #1

I take my father's nose and shove it in a box.
My mother's mouth lays claim to the vowels

of my making. I learned to tend and till and dig

and there is something like a hole where a good
family should be but instead I have the good people

who did the best they would with what they had.

I've learned the salt of the earth art of settling,
my body fatigued, progeny of two small Mississippi towns,

their lightning bugs fat like dream songs trapped
in a mason jar. I forget to make holes to breathe.

Forget to say my father

when he says not mine, tests the blood or sweat laden bed.
I hate inferred language. We sift through the words and

let the sting silt through. In a dream, I was this brown
drowning in brown water. In a past life, I was a witch

with twenty gold bangles and choking on sand.
When I woke, I asked for a new father.

His wounds so welt and Black and man, him the most
country in a city in a country that tells him to forget he's alive.

He lifts the weight on his belt. He holsters the gun,
lighter than the double barrel shotgun he held to my mother,

under the bedsheet damp with sex, until on to the next wife,
his inherited daughters, built a house safe as a prison,

his finger smooth on the trigger. There are all kinds
of intimate violence. I am no dummy. He is a good man.

How the words crawl into the nook in the back of my knee.

How the It sidles close to the hairs on the nape. Sometimes
it pools and pulls, sometimes is a daughter trying

to understand a man's hard silence, how it chokes.

Turns a ghost into a haint: humming. Becomes
a blood song. Sometimes I am still the girl making angles

of her body, jabbing elbows into him like hammers,
when I loved wrestling and wanted to be a boy.

He'd say to my mother be patient, how he won't raise
no punk ass girls which meant become a woman who can

change her own oil and tire and tell a man to jump into a river
until the day you need him to come home.

FEAR LEAVES BEHIND ITS OWN LIE

When the thieves popped off his wife's new
hubcaps, sat the shiny machine on bricks,

my father kept his gun near Hollering *Who
Is It* from the other side of the door

inside a gate behind another door It's late
when I return, three times I shout my name

between the deadbolt's slow slide From behind
bars on every door across every window,

except the living room, where one might, over warmed
day-old coffee, take note the wild-fat pheasant straggling

in the yard The neighbor pruning back what chokes her
glories And no, not even when her window glittered across

the grass, when the bullets did their death-dance
after her husband closed the pawn shop late

did my father move A man of men who clamored
for land they could pass down as genes Who wished

for sons Settled for daughters who might bring home
husbands who could *rope a tree trunk to their back*

but not speak of want without a drink doing its duty
Hold *immune from the risk of mental illness*

like a resigned lover Hold *Slaves could not own property*
enough to know desire can drive a man mad

A man who believes he's free: mad hatter We dress
it in cornmeal, lay it in hot oil, surprised by the sting

scarring our wrists The remedy sometimes the injury too
that crawls into our beds at night like a prophecy we ignore

DOES IT MATTER WHO IS YOUR REDEEMER

since the wired-eyed man couldn't tell our home from the crack house next
door: white as base when real good or dingy as aunt nora when she rolled
back that rock The raggedy kids next door, always uninvited A rusted car
grumbled and muffled them away For every flick'd pipe-flame, their mother
spit out a pearl Their daddy's greasy willows stuck to his days-stained shirt
Through windows, wind snow sleet I'd hear them suckling that love affair
until he smacked that then smacked her around Mema said she knew it was
coming: the night glass groaned crash, my mother's *fire* became *higher, higher*!
I tried to pull beyond that loam of sleep, out of a grave vision Stretched my
arms into brown vines crawling through the pitch, flames bright and hot as
angels Crackle ashed our house clean My mother drug my limp-woke body
down the drive like impatience is a virtue approximate to flight And fight
How long it took to quash her rage: waiting on the engine men Waiting
for my father For rain Mema says prayers need feet I count on my toes to
ten, ten times til our house becomes a missing tooth in the night's mouth

II

WHEN THE THERAPIST ASKS YOU TO RECOUNT, YOU HAVE TO SAY IT

We chewed June between gulps of cheap
sugary drinks, walked the gauntlet of ogs[1],
sneakers slick beneath hems of creased jeans
laid flat against their pulse as they watched
the parade of women, dresses stretched as skin,
hair laid and flipped, honey, mosquitoes gnawing
on the sweet sweat pooling between breasts, after
always, having been ground against by a stranger
wanting our number slid into their front pocket, hands
lingering along seams Or, it happened, having pushed
the hands of each og away from my ass demanding
a space to twerk against the damp fog rising above
the dance floor, feeling the DJ's down tempo,
commanding more wind girl more *yeah* girl
And it happened, feeling a rogue breeze dry beads
across the nape, a grip on my arm wants to know
if I'd had children, my body made ample for feeding,
licked his lips while his eyes traced the circumference
of curves lying beneath my low cut, who I pulled away

[1] Og (n): a predator with no specific gender performance

from with no further words who yelled across the deck
beyond the crowd *nappy-headed bitch* beyond snickers
pointed fingers shook heads It starts this way Makes
you travel in a pack at night Keep your coat on
It's the same face outside the locker room,
on the tv screen His broad against me against
the hardwood banister, *titties* and *tight pussy*
crawling up my skin It happened while I thought
about grace, how a lady handles her body How
a flipped finger or fist might invite snatch-back
while walking to the bathroom alone, walking
to the car alone it happens, having *no business*
putting yourself anywhere in the world they say
is how you become the *kind of woman who learns*
when to shut up and take it

INTAKE INTERVIEW

Have you witnessed or been affected by violence? If yes, explain

Before the gunshots rang, us rum dumb,
a girl stripped on the dance floor.

Skirt pulled up above every hipwind
against the first by a second's hands:

never had coke or ecstasy,
but learned to loose the last drop

from the bottle with the best of them,
spliff & drag, muscles made numb

who is the victim of witness,
to crave and swallow the knowing.

Remember the thick Tallahassee heat
rubbed against our bodies in the field?

Hungry are the ogs[2], the witnesses,
the chorus *let that hoe know, let that hoe*

know echoing across the crowd & when
he exhales from his jeans

thrusts into her uptempo
no one turns away Some

cheer, some rigid with shock, soles
planted on the floor Instead we pull

cell phones from pockets, catalogue Fear
they might forget every detail after,

casually to a friend say *I was there,*
you won't believe we never thought to

ask her name

[2] Og (n): a predator with no specific gender performance

Have you   *violence? If*   *explain*

before the gunshots rang, rum done,
girl stripped on the dance floor,
he offered me a spliff, though
never asked my name. Us in the woods,
me against trunk, hard bark veins filling
with the skin of my back, surrounded
by too many trees to feel safe, glistened
by the Tallahassee heat, a split tongue that could slice
me down the middle Desired a ruinous
love, I settled for what I asked for: be wanted
The first casing fell soft like a stunned lightning
bug across the ground I was drug into
the pavilion for safety
I wanted the story to write itself:
me grateful to know my place,
find a hero who never thought to ask my name

or   affected   violence?   explain

I'm trying to unlearn it all, drawers
on nightstands, tucked in my purse
a mouth full of palmetto bugs,

pink empty belly, wet
lungs brown with newly burned-green
that damned heat warming red dirt

Crows there, too
cawing like clockwork every morning,

the wet ground and the fat worm
that writhes toward the light

How to say *sorry for believing I was different*
than the half naked girl
and the first and second og,
and the hands pressed
against keys, archiving

How all of us blamed the rum, or the ecstasy,
or the spliff coating our lungs, and the heat too
soaking tree limbs

Us running from the fields
toward corners of the pavilion after
the gun pointed at the black sky
emptying hollow point chatter
against dewed grass?

I know it happened this way
I went home to sleep
and lie

been   by, violence?   explain

Forget the og
Slipped pants on the floor

Forgot the girl's name you never asked,
        dawn-quiet, cross-legged in the dewed grass

Forgot the man who waited on the dark stoop
after he walked you to each door

Forgot the hand he held as the salt stained your good shirts

        Forget his mouth pulled thin with rage,
        Imagined fists that bludgeoned open the og's body,
        a face of ground meat like some kind of justice

Forgot the machine that held your mother's lilt,
        imagine you told her and she came knocking
        with a pot of collards,
        her sparrow-heart in her hands

Forgive the woman with glass lips and patent-strappy heels
  Forgive her leaving you Forgive you leaving too
  Forgive the wolves inside you and the fire ants
  swelling the poison out

Forgo lightning bugs in your name: how your
  mother spelled it to lift,
  To be alpha and omega
  To punch and sit up ask:

having to admit that/ i really was a girl &/ all of a sudden was orchid and ochre and obsidian and oak hued children we were not small but without our mothers was bus at a safe speed down the dark road us in the dark woods lamp posts tall as flags lit only a short distance was our hands harnessing the medallion glow of plastic cups emptied of 100 proof was punch into our sweat-glistened bodies was the thickly rolled spliff and its orange corona was the tree and scaled skin pressed into there or was a boy between my body the tree speaking nothing of consequence was time buffering, loading beneath the thick Tallahassee heat and too, the gunshots done was our humid fog consuming the pavilion was a new juke joint, shadow hotbox

         is this 100:

         a girl was [do I remember her face my face our faces]
         skirt slid up on was dance floor above
         each sip against one og by the second og's hands
         was hunger or witness in chorus *let that hoe*
         know, was *let that hoe know* echoing
         the chamber was the cough [his face
         his face and his face too] released himself
         from starched denim was a slip of history of violence
         thrust hungry inside her

we didn't turn away
cheering rigid in shocked-glee
soles dead Root be sweet now
darling grotesque is Cover your
eyes for more is a catalogue for
fear they might forget Us in the
details causally to a friend *was*
there you won't believe we never
thought to ask What was her name

CONSENT IS A LABYRINTH OF YES

1   For boys on the playground who master grab and run

2   For the friend's father who stood stoic in the doorway,
asks you to stay, television glow casting shadows across his face

3   For a grandfather whose hands blur toward the youngest in the dark and

4   Grabs your breast at the kitchen table or

5   A grandmother removes him from the scene by his collar, beats him
with his own cane or

6   The family *almost* talks about it and

7   The women kneel for prayer *Protect mine, O Lord, for they do not know
what is not their fault*: to have a body that can take and spit life back
out and

8   For the only lover who said no after too much gin and

9   For the og[3] who preferred you that way

10 She becomes a woman for the first time and again
     when she takes what she wants to, so

11 She never wants to have children Not that way or any way,
     and doesn't, since

12 History is a dangerous legacy of

13 *Learning* he says

14 A woman digs up her name from her throat The water
     washes out the mouths of what came before

15 A grandmother triggered back to her body: blued, locked
     in a room Her daughter remembers the double barrel aimed
     at her naked after making love The child has already coaxed
     a silence she did not know was hers to keep

16 Nothing stands still Starkness and light Her salt body, shadow
     and shimmer Her afraid but not yet done not yet

[3] Og (n): a predator with no specific gender performance

JOURNEY TO THE GARFIELD PARK CONSERVATORY WHILE READING "THE RED POPPY"

Convinced the lush green could hush
the static between my ears I wait
for the train to curve me toward
glass rooms thick with humidity & fauna

On the platform a man offers pocket-worn mints
from his ashened hands *No thank you si-*
and already I'm a stank-mouthed bitch

It's only Sunday It's not even dusk Soon I'll touch
the Carnauba Wax & Scheelea palms soaked in
hand-me-down light *The great thing is not having*
a mind as the doors snapped open between cars,
jerks the mint-giver back-and-forth like a doll
While the car swells with the scent of piss

Feelings: oh I have those A passenger
in his elbow-patched-tweed shifts
Uncrosses and recrosses his legs
His nose keeping the book's spine

from snapping shut
Did you
Permit yourselves
to open once

I have so little to give
Trace the page as he shuffles,
sits inches from my face, scream-asking
IS YOU A REAL NIGGA
IS YOU A REAL NIGGA until he's out of breath

At California, the passenger
abandons me for the next car

I press my finger into the page
Soften against the hard seat
Sir I don't know if I am though
I wanted to tell him where to find
the 70 graceful fronds from around
the world, cycads older than us

and I wanted to ask
how long he's been here
which year drove him over
or showed a vision of the world afire

Ask if he knows about the house in my dreams
where the keys chime on the walls
So frequently, they feel like a warning

But he fans me off and exits
between cars The tracks
rattle beneath the rocking

I speak
because I am shattered
Shit, me too

Me too

WHAT YOU KNOW ABOUT THAT
INTERSECTED LIFE

It's snake tongue flick back,
it's unfinished apple About
the murder of crows in the wake
of a good first moan Which
alley to steer clear, what come
back to avoid clap How to forget
the stirrups and saltines, the solemn
man who took them out You don't
know unending grief Spreading the
blinds when a lover's engine hums low
About the anchor in the swell of a belly
when the sirens flash Flashlight tap
against a window Strip search on a traffic
violation, a clerical error What you know
about the metal around wrist if it ain't
missionary, ain't spicing things up on
a Tuesday night What Detroit smells
like in summer: meat, burned brush,
fish flies dead, all too far from the river
Say a grandfather on a four-legged
cane sneaks into your room at night

Makes you want to holler Throw up both
your fists Say he blocks the exit
til a praying grandmother comes
Say her hymns be memory, aluminum
cracking against his skull Say it's
a story the cousins laugh about over
Thanksgiving dinner Out of his mind
just in time What you know about
deliverance About this badshit
in the brain and no prescription to take
What you know about water folding
back into itself, returning Returned

III

YOU NEED[ED] ME

"The graduate [Tiarah Poyau, 22] student who was gunned down at a New York Caribbean culture festival was allegedly murdered after telling a man to stop grinding against her."-Dailymail.com (09.7.2016)

The lie comes early Die a little at a time or Hush be dead You nothing but
treble Ignore the smoke when the bassline drops *come on baby*
into the void Once, then an echo *Get off me Don't*
sparks until a forest is on fire Climate emergencies barely get
top airwaves Why bus stops and train platforms The It
in boardrooms back alleys bars Our short birch lives twisted
in stagnant imagination My father says what he means *You*
think too much, got a mouth on you like a gun That was
a warning or we take metaphors too far Look I'm asking, just
trying to unhinge this power-logic gap How safe: sadity: another
lit match Spread your bark, give your tinder nigga
fix your face Why you ain't smiling filled with grace We tick on
barely a line in the segment on "gun violence" I buy a plane ticket to the
Atlantic, face my fear in private Fog but no Xanax Klonopin No moon hit
Not a cricket juke to get me right There are infinitudes I can list
in my daily anxiety mostly Men: following breathing asking why I'm tryna
be where I need to be on time & alive I don't know how to undo this fix
Burnt out, having to map out which exit is your savior your

captor Ask a patriot, politician, pastor or any inner
patient if they've loved a Black Woman beyond her verb Issues'
first definition is revenue My body transactional I want an exit with
a clear view home Want to be left alone Unbothered Draped in a
coat sumptuous as a late autumn sun emboldening red leaves, I mean *bad*
like: *come through* Like: death can't be the proof I'm only a bitch
still willing to love you

MARY WOODSON SETS THE GRITS STRAIGHT

They remember the clumped hot

grain burning breakdowns into his back,

his comeback to God Third-degree salvation

Through word of mouth I'm his Wife Girlfriend Lover

Who gets it right The pistol's click-down

til the hole blew open a way to say *no, not today*

You crazy for that one Mary Which door we enter through

Museum of dollar store dames Thrift fur and wrong

diagnoses Light wanderers through wrought iron gates

Who needs who when legends need a fix Forget us

until we're dead Revised inaccurate if written at all

Paranoid peony Pen us songs to sit us up right

Make me happy baby, weave your cry down

in your bones, let me sing baby crazy I can't leave

your love alone Crazy which door threw: archway,

rot iron gait, nails bruised at the beds, scarlet and slick

Was I scratching my way to the beginning?

Not his heard-degree burn

click down of the pistol's clamor, they said

he wanted me to be his knife, his whirlfriend

A hole enough to let the static out We rarely

strut through the front dour Often, men

believe we have the keys to unlocking every ghost

they can't bear to face

HUMORISM

Night-alone in the beautiful borrowed house I vow never to watch another
horror film Where the woman squeaks a dish clean sings braless between
Joplin's threshold-throat, pleads *lord work* not to leave her down here in
it She's a bow on a handsaw, thin and tinned, her water on metal cutting
through Birch limbs drop appendages of pine cones, mimic ghost-fists on a
dinner table The driver says *What a perfect place to be murdered* and laughs
Outside, the deep-seated sea skirts its fog-hem just beyond the dim glow of
porch light I am almost always afraid Little humor in the tea leaves Almost
always a body of little lemon pills to sleep or swim in it Suck the songs back
when Sandra and Renisha and Korryn Sleep comes and does good or the
fitful dreams scatter like black mollusks along a Massachusetts shore The
hole keeps our music all horse hair pulled taut on the wind-bough-bend
with teeth It's cool, keep it Rinse the silver pans until they creak and moan
Wipe the counters smooth Tuck in Keep a night stand light on Be a mother-
figure with a maldescent faucet to drink from Be the bridge rot breakable,
no discernable beam left Click down quick Switch back Don't say her Say
her name, a wish that maybe you'll say mine Inferred punch Line break Bone
broke Say it I dare you

BEFORE I FIRE HER, THE THERAPIST ASKS *WHAT IS IT LIKE TO BE A BLACK WOMAN HERE*: A MONOLOGUE

after Ross Gay

I love your hair You always wear such interesting things What did you do before this Wow are you from Detroit What was that like Tell me what your thesis is about That sounds really powerful Your poem tonight was really intense You'll appreciate this, you know, since you're kind of ghetto You worked so hard you made it So what did you think about that Junot Díaz essay I'm suspicious of poems with an agenda, that have a certain aboutness Explain what you mean when you say risk I'm really uncomfortable I went to Detroit Well Dearborn, and it's amazing how cheap the houses are No, it's a really cool town Are you a Tigers fan That city is having a hard time, for sure I lived there once when I worked for Teach for America How do you feel about people who claim Detroit but aren't really from there I really love your hair Is your work always so intense That line is a little melodramatic I'm not as smart as you but I thought rape was about sex What do you mean it's hard to date I mean you're here Rap is about music let's not make it about race Oh come on, I only call people I love my nig— I don't mean this to sound racist—You don't seem like you date white guys bu— I love how our skin looks when I hold your han— I like women who live a natural lifestyle You're so well spoken Wow you've really read a lot Ithaca must be way different than what you're used to You can breathe now, you made it

ALWAYS SOMETHING HERE
TO REMIND ME

I face myself when I hear the news
Driving toward the mall to buy the kind

of camouflage it takes to be a woman
say *I'm good* The summer mild-long,

my sister still warm in her grave

I feel most dead these days, grief a tick
latched at my neck I am most lonely

when I feel this dead In the parking lot
the engine runs The podcast hosts press

I am so fucking tired, I'm tired of being
peaceful I'm tired of this shit What else
do we have to do to be treated human?

A woman slows her walk toward her mini-
van, my volume full blast She winces

I realize how hard I'm sobbing I don't
recognize my sound I don't wipe my face

I walk inside, tell the counter-woman without
looking *NW 47 and the blot powder*

in deep dark Please And when she *no, no*
that can't be right, you're much lighter than that,

I stare And she stares and waits And I stare, say
nothing and we go on like this under the flickering

fluorescence until she retrieves a foundation
two shades lighter, opens it, taps it on a mirrored disk,

dabs her sponge And she doesn't ask before reaching
And I don't pause before grabbing her wrist

Just Get Me What I Asked For And she stares
and I stare, the lights still buzzing and maybe

I haven't been dead but living in this second stage
of grief, this rage that drops its red hot pin on a map:

Missouri, Michigan, Florida, New York,
Mississippi, California Where I look for other

words for meadow marrow crow I want more
than what I get Where there are no more black dresses

or mothers with carnations pinned to their blouses
No causes and no news outlets to say alleged

when they mean deserved it In a different world
I don't have to face myself I don't take a white lover

only to take something back I pull into the driveway
on a safe tree-lined street Set my bags on the counter

My lover texts *How are you?* I type his name like a prayer
Michael Michael Michael Michael Michael

Who? she asks *Who?*

EVERYTHING'S ASK PLEASE
DON'T FINE ME

I wake early to wash the wild dirt

from my hair Instead check my timeline

to find a country not mine says

it's legal for everyone to pretend

at being a little less lonely if they want

I smoke on my porch swing while

an ole easy-like-Sunday-morning rat

strolls down the sidewalk of

my gentrified life It's funny what

you get used to mid-drag Shut

the gray day behind me make a fresh

pot of coffee Where are the tweezers

to pluck wires from my chin Which

wires do I dial at the HRC to ask

them what they did for Shelley

Hilliard's mother If they could identify

her child's body burned, in pieces

amongst uncut grass Maybe I'll braid

or two-strand twist into happy

Forget between shoveled forks of seitan

most women who want to fuck me are

internet activists who wish I'd just spend

the night It's Friday & someone will throw

a party with more red wine than whiskey

Can I stain my teeth for the summer

I promise I'm trying to be more happy

I might pay my rent on time and not think

about the student loan debt crisis I try

to wrangle these roots respectable but

this mourning keeps getting in my way

ONE BLUES IN THE HAND GOOD AS SEVERAL IN THE BLOOD

Having not chopped but brought in the wood,
stacked the hunks into a monument for burning

Having scrubbed the mollusks to gleam,
having browned them open, seasoned a bath

that would wash away any shame to run from
Sponge the milky brine with garlic'd bread brushed

with oil: of ripe olives from the long rows of trees
I did not pluck from or grow I know what

it means to be lucky and alive to suck out the pit
Gather the clef, leap in the go-go of a good day

Harken a lineage: third descendant of Roxie Morris: of
mechanic garb smeared in crude and sweat, cranking

wrench beneath: fire crown of auburn nap and freckle:
architect of spades games, full plates and easy shade:

of cuss your children out for sawing her good dining room
chairs with the steak knives: of migration and leaving

husbands: of one blues in the hand is as good as several
in the blood: who escape novel death: the lucky and

scarred colliding like genres, genes: of those who love
too much A well Archive of my heart A wonder in winter

dirt colding over consequence Waiting, green, budding
and bursting Women of sequin tatter, sunrise's hem

and haw—light rising as buttered cornbread
—skimming gold off the anxious water

STILL LIFE OF ACME IN SPRING

for francine, for Detroit

From my mouth, forgive me: friend, woman
When I said there are no flowers here, I forgot
to mention the bloom of lace around a young girl's

ankle at Easter, her peony-shaped afro puffs,
carnelian carnations pinned to dresses honoring
those mothers not lost Spectrum of May collected from

Eastern Market, rowed in mismatched rainbows
in red wagons or inside the phantom box of a son's
arms I forget the cured meat spread out from the black

barrel of a barbeque, bushel of yarn sopped with sauce,
unlike the gauze full of blood from a young boy's head
Dear God the plankton of music dying our faces in the hot

summer streets, fever of jazz, blush of blues: raw heart
confront me This city, always in my face Bouquet of
incense, apothecaries with shea and oils Give a dollar

and I'll show you a conductor, his white bucket symphony
No I haven't forgotten the fire, molotov shards spreading
orange and gold flames as a field of dahlia across our

living room licking my mother's heels, the heroine wolf
dragging me from my bed I don't blame the addict
who didn't know which house to huff and blow down,

or the firemen arriving late And yes, angels too
A neighbor who let me, knees pressed to sternum, watch
from his porch as our house ashed itself clean We have

to see the truth of things Did I say there was no flora here?
No pollen shaken from the anther's round head,
the yellow dust settling in the cracks of windshield?
I meant: give me a plot I'll dig to the rich black

IV

GO HERE NOTHING TO SEE HOME

the bitch barks in the dark yard

of an old dream before the molotov

crashed through my sleep when I

tell the story people's eyes widen

like hard-boiled eggs elsewhere

I had a slinger they said was my father

not sure if my brain latched to lore

or I caught like a moth some utterance

between the women who made me

over coffee his hands big enough to

gather the collar of my mother's jacket

drag her out the car door I've always

suffered from terrible sleep my gift

to see through the walls of ogs I wake

wet and shivering a new worm in a fresh

body a child screaming for the end in the

morning I search the newspapers for their

name, syllables broken at the hands of

someone they loved how the news comes

frenzied like that scared bitch yelping

helpless at lightning and drums when men

ask me for water I know they mean my pussy

though they bring no buckets or even

a small glass often I lay my dress

across their mouths, pour and wait to see

which one won't drown it's the closest

I've come to love though that's not the right word

HINDSIGHT

the potted lily was a horrible gift
but you should have seen your face, excited

you found a keepsake, something
to root my name, keep the delicate coo

when we made love, living it was easy

in the beginning: coddle each bud, every
drop swelled, found its way down

into the rich earth months passed
we pretended we could make ourselves

familiar, ignored the wounds,
their slender open mouths after you left

I moved it to the floor, sat on the edge
of the bed, watched the stems limp

over and split down into the dry dirt
the roots, small like empty veins

FAILED REINCARNATION
BEFORE OLANZAPINE

My honeycomb illness of bees buzzing
bright in the brain, their sticky spittle
turning hours in kaleidoscope
that slow-drip, the trees' autumnal gold...
How it latches to the shoulders of pedestrians,
like the *take me with you* of lovers
Take me across the thresh of whichever door
might amp this song up, good needle jitter
When the station's stuck between suffer
and c'est la vie, who in a body like this
can afford to believe in reincarnation, though,
once I dreamed a river of mercurial silt and gold
bangles bridging over my opened wrists
And the sun's radial rippling despite
rising brown water Here language in limbo,
of leveraging one evening for a hush
if you can manage A whisper taut or torch
or touch can bind you to a fever if unchecked, let
Wound then bruise renders blues inevitable
From the green porch I swing between the whir
of dissolving cars that whip and exhale Panic

pitters its baseline like a house track Begs:
dance dance dance dance Asks if you believe
in a God who demands to witness
what worship wild abandon becomes

WHEN WE SAY WE WANT TENDERNESS
WE HAVEN'T FOUND A PUNISHMENT
WE CAN LIVE WITH

Careening between cuffing seasons, I let
myself be good a sinner Our tongues
tussle between this three am fog and nothing
is miraculous about our bodies except our petulant
hunger You my one-off lover massage my
calloused feet and we fill the dusk with nothings
Feign intimacy It's all fine and dark and I push
your face deep enough into my water, pretend this is
what desire feels like But oh, what the clit will do
to remember a collaborative song, its greedy tenor
I am no different than any other animal and the lies
we tell: when we say we want tenderness we mean
we haven't found a punishment we can live with
When I say cup the stretch marked meat, slap
the hip's horizon until it vibrates the highest pitch,
I mean let's make a terrible love song in which
I mean there is no love in conquest in which I say
I'm sorry for the acquisition committed by this
lonely and how I wish I wanted to take it back

ROOT WORK

You watch as I take
each section of dread,
wet at the root It is winter
I press olive oil into loose
strands, twist between finger
and thumb into palm, then
palm and roll into brown reeds
You ask if you can try, just
this once Say you want to help
You *oh*, breathe slow and heavy,
watch this work Late morning
light bends through blinds, all
my tools spread out around me:
metal clips, rattail comb, bottle
of lavender water set to wide-spray
On this plot, I want to keep specific
rituals to myself, where one unlocked
gate won't access the lot You click
to another station on the tv
Like silence is the only brutal thing
you do Last night you tucked in
deep, called me Queen, satisfied

you found a space to try *Just this once*
and I shut off the lamp, press against
the edge of the dark Certain voices
I am not willing to carry At half moon,
I bleed heaviest when you want
me most Drunk on every story heard:
to be bound At dinner, my scarf tied tight
until the shiny stalks are dry, you push
around small clots of tomato, disappointed
by the cheap fruit I emptied from the dusted
can, careful not to risk one
slipped blade, one thin slice of meat between
knuckle or from the tip Three bowls in,
You're still hungry I light a cigarette
as the truck outside revs its engine
and dies You wave away my smoke
curled around your face, tap
the up-arrow on the control,
until you find a station more your speed,
where all the men wear backward snap-
backs and drink cheap beer You mention
preta, that we should aspire to live
a life of holy suffering The prayers of men
There is a spell for everything

V

NOCTURNE WITH DARK HONEY

I burned the last of our summer

beneath the new moon Gathered

small offerings: a jar of nails dug up

from the wet yard, five dried rose petals,

an empty

bordeaux bottle, dregs of dark honey

The neighbor let out the dog, voice

so hushed her *why* smaller than a mole

Sirens blare blocks over

I turn the match on its head Strike

No matter the hour or years we are

all this sleepless, busying our hands

with someone to save. Or kill.

I lit the map we made

of partial spells, instructions

on how or when to crawl

from inside the dark's dark

Between dreams

you warned *I could bleed any moment*

In one my mouth was a stream, then

a river There was a swell and

a sea came bearing every name

Desire is a leash I gladly

fail to break my beasts well

and the gods we make

The last morning's coffee with cayenne

The loud-bright walk

home, behind me our limbs

tangled at the wind's mention

And the song in your throat

Lowhum A gossamer

ghost I swallowed,

without flinching

AUBADE WITH DARK HONEY

Without flinching Ghost I swallow

Lowhum gossamer in your throat

    At the wind's mention   home,

    behind me our limbs tangled,

the loud-bright walk

    our last morning's coffee with cayenne

      The gods we made

I know my beasts well

Desire, a leash I gladly fail

A sea came bearing

every name A river

There was a swell then

In one my mouth was a stream,

then I could bleed *any* moment

Between dreams you warned,

from inside the dark's dark

On how or when to crawl

out of partial spells, instructions to save or kill

I lit the map

We something with our hands Years

Are we all this sleepless, busying

no matter the hour or strike?

Turn the match on its head and sirens blare

blocks over A *why* smaller than a mole,

so voice, hush the dog

The neighbor let out dark bottle honey,

dregs of bordeaux,

the wet yard,

five dried rose petals,

an empty

A jar of nails dug up

from gathered offerings

Small Summer

Our beneath

The last of a moon

I burned new

I GOT MAD LOVE

There's no Drew Barrymores in my
adaptation Lovers watch me spin into
snow lines of static, leave with the front
door open Couldn't cut out the eyes
of magazine girls, paste them blue
to the wall Watch tutorials on how
to crown locs electric I've bruised men
without permission Masturbate before
dressing for work, beat my face for the gods,
keep a good purple eyeliner in the clutch
Sit in traffic, punch a clock smile like I own
a thing or two When bleeding, drink beet
juice Pray for a reason to clap back, laugh
too loud Call it joy or pay a bill on time Pretend
memory is not a hangover Find a cure Viola Davis
through a room with no wig Call a bigot, bigot
Keep hunger for push, fingers against the wall of
necessary writhing I'm feeling myself
on the dance floor in the bedroom of my witching
hour Light the mother's candle, hope I don't salt
to ground I hope Eat collards out the pot, drink
its liquor Let my body welt from today's blue pleasure

Don't look for Chris O'Donnell to save me,

he was a shitty Robin anyway It's not the 90s anymore

Except for this matte, the way I rip my jeans

Some days I am brave, walk to the train without headphones

Wish somebody would tell me to smile, the arrow of brow

cutting their spleen out Come home Take this sheer black

bra off before the deadbolt slides shut

Pour myself a glass of red wine, let it stain my tits

Roast a chicken and suck the salt off every finger   Live

SANCTI SPÍRITUS

Trinidad, Cuba: 2017

Rain commas the coming dusk

    as we wander cobblestone streets that sweat, steam

    along gated windows where old women

        recline in front of box televisions

    or stand in doorways gossiping back and forth

        until the bread cart's bell chimes through

            their arms triangled on one hip

        In Yemaya's house the walls white

    though not maleficent, zaffre waves draped

so close to the ceiling I wade through an old, heavy memory

shepherded by a priest draped in beads

who only speaks with his eyes We enter, wait to touch

archives, photographs of ceremony glued to faded pages

parades of gorgeous people

all invocation of sun, unfettered for a moment

We hear two dogs fight outside the barred window,

then a survivor's yelp A streak of scraggly refuge

barks at C's feet and curls beside her to rest

The priest still says nothing, though he knows

whose daughter she is on this side of the veil

I offer three nacional to the altar

patron an answer to the dream lodged deep

in the channels of my body

Tomorrow we renegade to the beach

I walk into the sea, let the salt seed

 in the reeds of my hair And maybe this is a kind of

 drowning I believe in Thick and slow

Until, I let myself down into myself into current into

 babel and swell into my old good name

BREAKBEAT NOCTURNE WITH ANEMONES AND LUCKY FISH

February fever   and the body begs deliverance

In line women teem   with brink, shudder against

the shrill season, ecstatic   coronas piercing through

the veils between us   I give up my name and pay nothing

descend into the mouth   of the club where cumbia

slips off my thick coat   You flit between floors, green rooms

beneath yellow street lights   high off echolocation,

chest warm with menthol   the heat of our need to come

I center my hips   in the crowd's nexus, conjure

a deep song Salt, so   sweat a sea of wild anemones

between your thresh   and breakbeat, maestro

of trap and tropical bass   I slither and bend into every note:

torso in translation,   pelvis sapid premonition,

bones drunk on steel   drum and hand clap What

is the body for if not this   black writhe of being alive

the sibilance we submit to   and the wild language of air

sucked between teeth   In the Grimoire of My Life

see: lucky fish, a thousand   questions curled as cowrie

Wants, rich   and how long, despite the world's

benevolent violence   I kept death waiting,

waiting, waiting and waiting

BREAKBEAT AUBADE WITH ANEMONES AND LUCKY FISH

Waiting and waiting, death I kept waiting Despite
the world's benevolent violence   Wants rich and long,

questions curled as cowrie See: a thousand lucky fish
          in the Grimoire of My Life The wild language of air

sucked between teeth and the sibilance we submit to
          Is the body not for this If   Black writhe of being alive

What steel-clap hand, drunk bones and premonition:
sapid pelvis in translation, torso of trap and tropical bass

I slither and bend into every note I slip maestro,
          between your thresh and breakbeat,
sweat a sea of wild anemones Salt, so a deep song

Chest warm with the heat
          of our need and the menthol to come

High off echolocation, lights yellow the streets
                    Beneath green rooms, I slip off my thick flit

Between floors cumbia mouths my name,
says descend in and pay nothing

      Give up the veils between us
             Ecstatic corona, I pierce

through the shrill season, against
             Shudder Teem brink

Woman in line
         with deliverance Fever

    And the February a body begs

WE LIVE BEST / IN THE SPACES
BETWEEN TWO LOVES

Trinidad, Cuba: 2017

Sun drunk and bruised we stop
for mango juice, so sweet it jolts the tooth
Chickens scurry beneath our legs, peck
at cartilage and scraps of bone C and J laugh
canibalismo Push cainito halves to the plate's ledge,
one for each of my palms Slow I thumb the pits loose,
cradle the etymology thick and viscous in the valley
of my tongue: purple star apple, golden leaf, abiaba,
pomme du lait, estrella, aguay, milk fruit My little lobe
glows warm and fat Curled around a blurred past life
Violet nights exhausting my dizzy tongue beside
offerings: stiff petals, moon blood and stone I've come
here to clear a vision of myself and let it be true
This useless imperial language with one word
for hunger One for thirst Ears pressed between veils,
straining to hold some silver ephemera not mine to keep

A LONGED-FOR, WHICH I
ENTER GRATEFULLY

for CO

Scraped slow with ink
I return, question what is
a symbol other than a con-
stellation of becoming we
debate which dogmas
can withstand the years
Your fingers like primas toe
fresh-hot scars with ointment until
we stand in one shadow spilled
against the late summer light
across your bathroom floor,
you: home when I am want
You salve like this&this & this
Light blinks us back to that Harlem
fire escape where we fired frenetic
cigarettes into the sun, talking
about our fathers, whether
the duende of making love is
capable without apparitions or

only constant in an omen's lap and
If we're dying for clarity these days
Veils are nimble, breach Bones grow
despite their feeble failure We ask
what ambient garble news is now,
touch for the act of touching,
my need for tenderness
so small it fits at the edge
of a fingernail, at the edge
of the fingernail's edge
At night we sleep
in the same bed, pull
breezes from our breathing
I only snore when it's safe
Know safe means sleep
close to likethis & too   this

BORN AGAIN ON A PILSEN DANCE FLOOR

Dervish of black pleather, chandelier of ink
latticed across my shoulder, I guzzle through

the tunnel of a straw, return to a lover
as percussion coaxes my ass into figure-eights

Traffic shuffles through the gangway
of the club A woman praises *yas hair flip* until

I am a cyclone of forgetting Mizuko in fish-
net conjures on top of the bar Fastens a metal

harness to her crotch, grinds against the machine,
bestows a cascade of sparks

Mizuko thrusts slow a waterfall of light across us
Mizuko makes it rain radiant from behind

The brilliance spills out, down her legs and
Look: I have left men for much less, more than likely

will do so again What animals back
into the shadow of their hunger

I bear my face to the falling andromeda,
press against the pyrotechnic

glory that threatens to set me on fire
Let her spray me down before December

embezzles me into the same old mistakes
Convinced I can be born again, every night,

exactly like this

MASTER OF MY MAKE-BELIEVE

I.

I spoke into the chamber of myself, and took back the derecho of my name.

II.

The goal then. Supremacy natural. As ritual. Longing a kissed thing. Which supposition. Exhausted question. Or none. Not if or if that imagination. Arrogant with fear. It takes a village to. Survive and confuse it with. Living. A history hellbent. Erasing. Burning. The state of nothings. Inference. Blank an unblanked breathing. Snuffed. Made ditch worthy, suffocated armature. Pressed. Limp. A fact blurred, the lie. The syllogism seared, inescapable. Can't body: future. Body past participle. Bagged. Typed over. Tinctured. In the molecule. Drink. Drink. Drunk. Hungover and echoed. Steered into then. Steel of it. Industrial soaked. Thirst.

Fatigue being the only word swelled beneath my tongue, I drank until each bud was plump. Spit-burst and slurring, I begged the next familiar lover. I am trying to unsee the need to be desired. Deny this country another glass of wine. I plate a whole bird, slathered in salt and butter. I wear my good dress and heels, tits perched as high as the crisped-brown breasts of this feast. And won't you try to ride me into your horizon of longing until the receding light is swallowed up? Out there, you keep your ideologies of God alabaster and dew-glistened. You dream of me. You hate your mouth for its water.

III.

But if we go, we go together.

NOTES

"In the Last Act, Olukún Reminds You of the Origin" receives a line from Betty Davis's song "They Say I'm Different," and engages Christina Sharpe's praxis *In The Wake: On Blackness and Being*.

"Hydrocephalus As a Misnomer for Water God" receives a line from Ibeyi's song "Think Of You."

"Between Heaven and The Most Southern Place On Earth" receives a line from Jerry Butler's song "For Your Precious Love."

"Fear Leaves Behind Its Own Line" receives lines from and is in conversation with the "Blacks Are Immune From Mental Illness" article by Dr. King Davis in *Psychiatric News* (May 1, 2018).

The fifth section of "Intake Interview" begins with a line from Pat Parker's "Goat Child."

"Journey to the Garfield Park Conservatory While Reading 'The Red Poppy'" receives lines from Louise Glück's aforementioned poem.

"You Need[ed] Me" is an end acrostic that receives a line from Rihanna's song "Needed Me."

Mary Woodson, a lover of soul singer Al Green, infamously scalded him with a pot of grits before taking her own life. Several "accounts" beyond the *NYT* 1974 article speculate she may have suffered from schizophrenia, though most "official" reporting speaks little of her life beyond her connection to Green. This poem receives lines from Al Green's song "Sha La La (Make Me Happy)."

"Humorism" lives with the murders of Sandra Bland, Renisha McBride, and Korryn Gaines.

"A longed-for, which I enter gratefully" receives its title from a phrase in Audre Lorde's "The Uses of the Erotic: The Erotic as Power."

"we live best / in the spaces between two loves" receives its title from a line in Tracy K. Smith's poem "A Hunger So Honed."

"Master of My Make-Believe" receives its title from Santigold.

ACKNOWLEDGMENTS

Many thanks to the editors at the following publications who had faith in these poems, from seed to root to branch:

Anomaly— "we live best / in the spaces between two loves" and "Breakbeat Aubade with Anemones and Lucky Fish."

Black Imagination— Where "a longed-for, which I enter gratefully" appears in its earlier, cross-genre version.

Buzzfeed & Furious Flower: Seeding the Future of African American Poetry— "When the Therapist Asks You to Recount, You Have to Say It."

The Collagist— "When We Say We Want Tenderness We Haven't Found A Punishment We Can Live With" and "Still Life of Acme In Spring."

DayOne— "everything's ask please don't fine me."

The James Franco Review— "I Got Mad Love," "Consent Is A Labyrinth of Yes," and "Before I Fire Her, the Therapist Asks *What IS It Like to Be a Black Woman HERE*: A Monologue," previously titled "Monologues In Bars By White People With Good Intentions."

Learn Then Burn 2: This Time It's Personal— "Between Heaven and the Most Southern Place On Earth."

Phantom Books— "What You Know About That [Intersected] Life"

Pinwheel Journal— "Master of My Make-Believe."

pluck!— "Always Something Here To Remind Me."

The Shade Journal— "Field Study #1."

Thrush Journal— "go here nothing to see home."

Union Station Magazine— "hindsight."

For your insight, questions, encouragement, meals, laughter, compassion, invitations, indelible care, and friendship, endless gratitude and light to: Phillip B. Williams, Justin Phillip Reed, Tarfia Faizullah, Christina Olivares, Krista Franklin, Emily Rose Kahn-Sheahan, Ben Clark, Miquela Cruz, Maya Marshall, Jayson P. Smith, Adjua Gargi Nzinga Greaves, Keith S. Wilson, avery r. young, Gala Mukomolova, anastacia-reneé tolbert, Kenyatta Rogers, Angela Fegan Davis, among a rich, serendipitous tribe of many more: bless.

My work exists in part due to the utterance, rigor, and expansive inquiry of the Detroit School, especially: Airea D. Matthews, francine j. harris, Tommye Blount, Nandi Comer, and always the late, great David Blair, who I miss beyond language, material-time, and worlds; our teacher (my forever-teacher) Vievee Francis, and comrades Scheherazade Washington and Tylonn J. Sawyer. Look at what we've done, do. Ever grateful for your work, love, kindness, and grit.

And yes you, Mr. Derrick Rogers, Sydney G. James, Jonah Mixon-Webster: bless. Blessed.

KMA Sullivan and YesYes Books: I never dreamed my work would end up in such incredible hands. Twice. Thank you for our beautiful journey, and for receiving me with such intention, warmth, and dedication.

Deepest gratitude to Cave Canem and Callaloo: when more than one stand in agreement, the world tilts on its axis. What you've given . . . a lifetime. A legacy. Thank you for what you've given, and what you continue to give. It'll forever burn on in this, in us.

Thank you to the Center for African American Poetry and Poetics, especially: Dawn Lundy Martin, Lauren Russell, and Terrence Hayes for investing into the future of Black letters, pedagogy and artistic dreaming.

And of those spaces, gifted with your beauty, I absolutely thank the following for their camaraderie, covering, and juke on the threshing floor: Khadijah Queen, Ladan Osman, Alison C. Rollins. What. Is. This. Beloved. Dream. Thank you for your generosity, for allowing space and believing. For your warrior-kinship. The world doesn't deserve any of us but should thank us all in the end.

Thanks to Cornell University's MFA program for providing time, space, and resources to think and ask through this work. To my teachers along the way: Lyrae Van Clief-Stefanon (immeasurable thanks, immeasurable gifts you've given, I'm so in debt to you), Dagmawi Woubshet (a rigorous dreaming, thank you), Carol Boyce Davies (radical considerations, and always, in awe of how you hold space): for guidance, some in more ways than I knew I needed, and some of which I got to turn on its head. And to Renia White, Evelynn Yuen, Harper Quinn, Emily Oliver, Kimberly Williams, Stevie Edwards, Matthew Reitger, Emma Catherine Perry, Mandy Gutmann-Gonzalez,

Richard LaRose: thank you for your keen eyes and furtive considerations, they'll stay with me, always.

To the Millay Colony, for the resources and quietude, those sweet coyote calls beneath the full moon, and for the following brilliant gifts: Carlos Syrah, Kyle Lucia, Natalie Smith, Anne de Marcken, and Anja Marais, for your mirroring, a now old-familiar song I hum daily.

Beloveds: Robert Martinez, Jr., Krystal Martinez, and Holiday, thank you for giving me a home with the kind of love to rise to. Thick.

To I.J., the best therapist and co-conspirator in this healing work: I would not have seen this book to completion without your radical support. Thank you for challenging me to lean in when self-love seemed too long, too far off in the offing. And no, none of these therapist poems are about you.

To my mama, Maria; mema, Franchella; great-gran Roxie: a long lineage of incomparable teachers, survivors, and warriors. Consider this a small offering in repaying my debt. My well deepens daily in your names.

PHOTO BY ROBERT MARTINEZ

ARICKA FOREMAN is a poet, editor and educator from Detroit. Author of *Dream with a Glass Chamber* (2016) and *Salt Body Shimmer* (YesYes Books 2019), she has received fellowships from Cave Canem, Callaloo, and the Millay Colony for the Arts. Her poems, essays and features have appeared in *The Offing, Buzzfeed, Vinyl, RHINO, The Blueshift Journal, Day One, shuf Poetry, James Franco Review, THRUSH, Please Excuse This Poem: 100 New Poems for the Next Generation* (Viking Penguin), among others. She lives in Chicago.

ALSO FROM YESYES BOOKS

Gilt by Raena Shirali

Boat Burned by Kelly Grace Thomas

RECENT CHAPBOOK COLLECTIONS

Vinyl 45s

    Inside My Electric City by Caylin Capra-Thomas

    Exit Pastoral by Aidan Forster

    Of Darkness and Tumbling by Mónica Gomery

    The Porch (As Sanctuary) by Jae Nichelle

    Juned by Jenn Marie Nunes

    Unmonstrous by John Allen Taylor

    Preparing the Body by Norma Liliana Valdez

    Giantess by Emily Vizzo

Blue Note Editions

    Beastgirl & Other Origin Myths by Elizabeth Acevedo

    Kissing Caskets by Mahogany L. Browne

    One Above One Below: Positions & Lamentations by Gala Mukomolova

Companion Series

    Inadequate Grave by Brandon Courtney

    The Rest of the Body by Jay Deshpande